# The Southwest

David Scott

## Consultants

**Brian Allman**
*Principal*
Upshur County Schools, West Virginia

**Devia Cearlock**
*Social Studies Coordinator*
Amarillo ISD, Texas

## Publishing Credits

Rachelle Cracchiolo, M.S.Ed., *Publisher*
Emily R. Smith, M.A.Ed., *SVP of Content Development*
Véronique Bos, *VP of Creative*
Dona Herweck Rice, *Senior Content Manager*
Dani Neiley, *Editor*
Fabiola Sepulveda, *Series Graphic Designer*

**Image Credits:** p5 NASA; p13 ZUMA Press Inc/Alamy Stock Photo; p16 Granger; p17 Library of Congress [98685386]; p19 (top) Library of Congress [LC-DIG-highsm-24969]; p22 Shutterstock/Mark Reinstein; p23 iStock Photo/JannHuizenga; p24 Christopher Brown/Polaris/Newscom; p25 Sarah Silbiger/Stringer/Getty Images; all other images from iStock and/or Shutterstock

## Library of Congress Cataloging-in-Publication Data

Names: Scott, David (David Coleman), 1971- author.
Title: The Southwest / David Scott.
Description: Huntington Beach, CA : Teacher Created Materials, [2023] | Includes index. | Audience: Grades 4-6 | Summary: "For thousands of years, American Indians occupied the Southwest. Then, Spanish and Mexican explorers and settlers arrived. The culture of the region was changed forever. Today, the Southwest embraces its rich American Indian, Spanish, and Mexican heritages. It also looks toward a future beyond the stars!"-- Provided by publisher.
Identifiers: LCCN 2022021243 (print) | LCCN 2022021244 (ebook) | ISBN 9781087691046 (paperback) | ISBN 9781087691206 (ebook)
Subjects: LCSH: Indians of North America--Southwest, New--Juvenile literature. | Southwest, New--Juvenile literature. | Southwest, New--Discovery and exploration--Spanish--Juvenile literature. | CYAC: Indians of North America--Southwest, New. | Southwest, New.
Classification: LCC F785.7 .S36 2023 (print) | LCC F785.7 (ebook) | DDC 979--dc23
LC record available at https://lccn.loc.gov/2022021243
LC ebook record available at https://lccn.loc.gov/2022021244

Shown on the cover is the Grand Canyon in Arizona.

This book may not be reproduced or distributed in any way without prior written consent from the publisher.

**TCM** Teacher Created Materials

5482 Argosy Avenue
Huntington Beach, CA 92649
www.tcmpub.com

**ISBN 978-1-0876-9104-6**
© 2023 Teacher Created Materials, Inc.

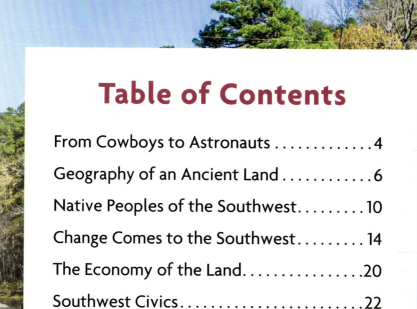

# Table of Contents

From Cowboys to Astronauts . . . . . . . . . . . . 4

Geography of an Ancient Land . . . . . . . . . . . 6

Native Peoples of the Southwest . . . . . . . . 10

Change Comes to the Southwest . . . . . . . . 14

The Economy of the Land . . . . . . . . . . . . . . 20

Southwest Civics . . . . . . . . . . . . . . . . . . . . . . 22

The Future Is Now . . . . . . . . . . . . . . . . . . . . . 26

Map It! . . . . . . . . . . . . . . . . . . . . . . . . . . . . . . 28

Glossary . . . . . . . . . . . . . . . . . . . . . . . . . . . . . 30

Index . . . . . . . . . . . . . . . . . . . . . . . . . . . . . . . 31

Learn More! . . . . . . . . . . . . . . . . . . . . . . . . . 32

Robbers Cave State Park, Oklahoma

# From Cowboys to Astronauts

The Southwest United States holds allure for many people. Much of the Southwest remains untouched. Monument Valley in Arizona has been featured in many movies because of its beauty and pristine nature. It is famous for its tall, red **buttes**. They have been the hideout of many Old West movie outlaws and the range for movie cowboys. No doubt, films have helped create a myth around the Southwest. But the Southwest is much more than what is shown on the screen.

The Southwest includes Arizona, New Mexico, Texas, and Oklahoma. These states were some of the last admitted into the United States. Today, much of the land of the Southwest belongs to American Indian tribes. Many people work hard to maintain the rich history and cultures of the native peoples.

Hunts Mesa in Monument Valley, Arizona

## The Future Is in Space

The Southwest is also the home of **Spaceport** America. This company is located in New Mexico. It is the world's first spaceport designed for commercial use. It has already launched more than 300 rockets! One day, anyone might be able to fly into outer space from New Mexico.

spacewalk training at the Neutral Buoyancy Laboratory

Astronaut Ellen Ochoa prepares for training at the Johnson Space Center.

The Southwest also looks toward the future. It is home to the Johnson Space Center. The center is located in Houston, Texas. It is where **NASA** astronauts train to fly into outer space. It has been the **mission control** for NASA space flights since the 1960s.

The story of the American Southwest is old. People first arrived in the area thousands of years ago. Its long story is one of loss, change, and hope for the future.

# Geography of an Ancient Land

People often think the Southwest is only desert. But the land of the Southwest is rich and **diverse**. It has mountains with ski resorts and a coastline with beaches. Parts of it are green with many trees and lakes. But the land did not begin this way.

Over 250 million years ago, a great sea divided North America in two pieces. In what is now New Mexico, the sea formed a great **reef**. Over millions of years, the water evaporated. The reef was buried, and the land rose. Rainwater seeped underground. It mixed with the limestone and formed the Carlsbad Caverns.

Carlsbad Caverns, New Mexico

## Ancient Mountains

The Arbuckle Mountains in Oklahoma are over one billion years old! When the mountains were formed, there was no life on the planet. Over time, the mountains have worn down and eroded, but they still stand. Water formed underground caves here like the ones in New Mexico.

Meteor Crater in Arizona

   Six million years ago, the Grand Canyon in Arizona did not exist. The Colorado River was just beginning to carve into the rocks. It took five million years to carve the canyon seen today. The lines on the walls show the history of the earth. It shows when oceans covered this land. It also shows when volcanic ash blanketed the area. The oldest layers in the canyon are from two billion years ago!

   Fifty-thousand years ago, Arizona looked very different. The temperature was cooler then. The ground was covered by woodlands. Mammoths and giant ground sloths fed there. From the sky, a giant meteor crashed into the ground. It made a crater 600 feet (180 meters) deep. This crater in the ground is visible today.

## Cultural Geography

The modern Southwest has a rich culture. It embraces its American Indian, Spanish, and Mexican **heritages**. People often think that cowboys are American. The truth is that many cowboy traditions come from the vaquero tradition of Spain and Mexico. *Vaquero* is the Spanish word for "cowboy." When the Spanish people arrived in the Americas, they brought both cattle and horses with them. Even the practice of cattle ranching came from Spain. This includes using **spurs**, **stirrups**, the **lariat**, and the **lasso**.

The official state sport of Texas is the rodeo. *Rodeo* is a Spanish word that means "round up." Rodeos are tests of skill. They include a lot of horse riding as well as contests for roping and handling livestock. These are all tasks performed on a cattle ranch. The first professional rodeo was held in Arizona.

rodeo rider

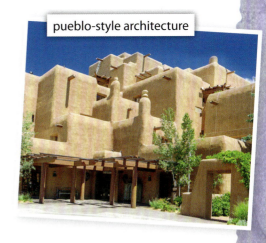
pueblo-style architecture

Pueblos are the buildings American Indians made out of adobe and stone. Some modern architecture in New Mexico is still built in the pueblo style. There are also buildings in the Southwest that are built in the old Spanish mission style. Since the 1960s, many homes have been built in a ranch style. The ranch style has its roots in the Spanish ranches of the 19th century Southwest.

Southwest foods also come from its past. Corn, beans, and **squash** are **indigenous** to Mexico. Many Southwest dishes use chili peppers that are grown in the region. Chili peppers are used in hot sauces. The original Tex-Mex foods served in the Southwest combine Spanish and Mexican dishes.

## Music of the Land

Music is often associated with an area of land. There are many different styles of music in the Southwest. Tejano music is one type. It came out of Texas. Tejano music is sometimes called Tex-Mex music. It combines Spanish vocals with polka or waltz music from Europe.

# Native Peoples of the Southwest

**Paleo-Indians** is the name given to the first people who lived in what is now the United States. They were mammoth hunters who followed large animals for food. They made tools such as spears and knives out of flint, a hard crystal rock. Their flint tools dating back thousands of years have been found in Texas. These tools show us that people have lived in the Southwest since before 13,500 BCE.

Today, we do not know much of the ancient history. The people did not record their stories for us to know today. But many ancient ruins can be found across the Southwest. They tell some of the story. For example, for at least 5,000 years, people have lived in Canyon de Chelly. We also know that the Hohokam peoples in Arizona built irrigation **canals** as far back as 600 CE. They farmed beans, squash, agave, and cotton. Over time, the canals have been buried under the desert floor.

American Indian arrowhead artifact

## Sunset Crater

In 1085, a volcano erupted in Arizona. The lava spread over 6 miles (10.5 kilometers). Volcanic ash fell over hundreds of miles away. The local Paleo-Indian tribes had to leave the area. Sunset Crater is just one of 550 volcanic vents in Arizona.

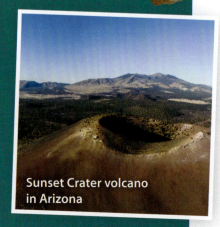

Sunset Crater volcano in Arizona

petroglyphs in Chaco Canyon, New Mexico

Pueblo Bonito ruins in Chaco Canyon, New Mexico

Around the year 900 CE, Chaco Canyon became a cultural center for the native peoples. It is located in New Mexico. People traveled from far away to meet there. They built giant buildings of stone and mud. Some of the buildings were used to keep track of sun and moon cycles.

The native peoples lived and thrived across the Southwest for many centuries. Their cultures were rich, and the people prospered. But explorers and settlers from elsewhere in the world slowly put an end to these early civilizations. Things changed dramatically when European people came to explore and settle the land.

## American Indians Today

While the civilizations of old fell, many native cultures are still thriving. Over five million American Indians live in the United States. They are a diverse people. There are 574 tribes in the United States. The people live on different lands. They speak different languages. They have different foods and **customs**. Most native peoples have moved to cities across the country, and they work in a wide variety of jobs.

But the native peoples of the Southwest keep their cultures alive through their languages, art, music, and traditions. Often, they gather together in celebration of their cultures. They take old traditions and bring them into modern life.

### Turquoise

American Indians of the Southwest often wear turquoise. For some American Indian cultures, turquoise represents good fortune, healing, and communication with the spirit world. Native peoples today may wear beautiful pieces of turquoise jewelry. Crafting such jewelry is an art.

## Gathering of Nations

An important part of some American Indian cultures today is the powwow. A powwow is an event where American Indians gather to celebrate their cultures. There is dancing, singing, and drumming. Contests are sometimes held.

The Gathering of Nations in New Mexico is the world's largest powwow. Over 700 tribes from North America participate. More than 72,000 people attend each year. It lasts for several days. The people share food, art, and music, and they socialize with each other.

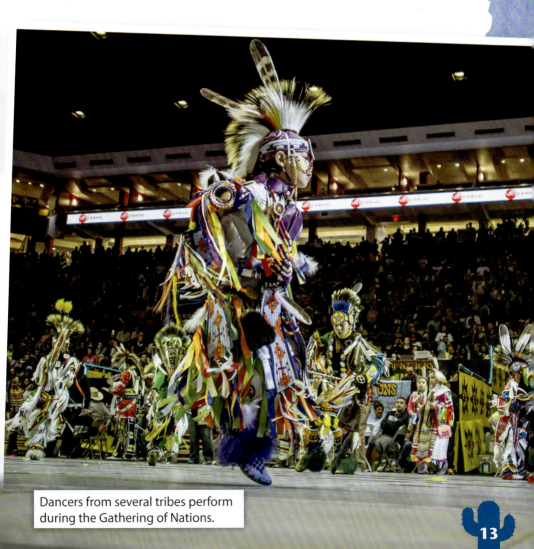

Dancers from several tribes perform during the Gathering of Nations.

# Change Comes to the Southwest

In the 1500s, leaders in many European nations wanted to find new trade routes and claim new lands. They sent explorers to the Americas. One European expedition started in 1540. The group of explorers was led by Francisco Vázquez de Coronado. He was a Spanish **conquistador** looking for a lost city of gold. More than 1,000 people came with him. They marched all the way from Mexico to modern-day Kansas. For two years, they explored the Southwest along the way. They were the first Europeans to see the Grand Canyon. But they could not figure out how to climb down to the Colorado River.

Coronado came across many native peoples on his path. Sometimes, he tried to befriend them. Often, he tried to conquer them and went to war against them. Many people died. And Coronado never found a lost city of gold, of course. It was only a myth.

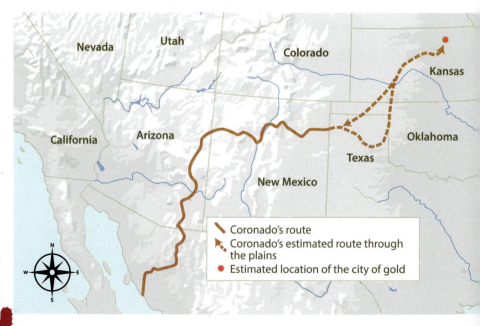

## Santa Fe

Santa Fe was founded in 1610 and is the capital of New Mexico. It is located 7,000 feet (2,133 meters) above sea level. It is the highest state capital in the United States. It is the second-oldest town in the United States.

Coronado left, but many of his people stayed in the Southwest. More Spanish settlers came as well. They brought food and animals from Spain. The Catholic Church built missions across the land and claimed it for Spain. They called it *Nueva España*, or New Spain. New Spain included not only the Southwest but also parts of the Caribbean and Florida. They enslaved American Indians at the missions. The native peoples were forced to work, learn Spanish, and adopt a new religion. The Spanish people also brought disease from Europe. The diseases were new to the native peoples, and they did not have **immunity** against them. Many American Indians died at the missions.

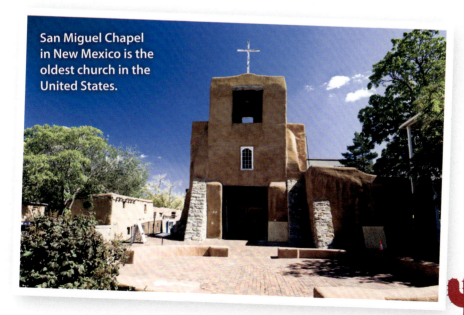

San Miguel Chapel in New Mexico is the oldest church in the United States.

## Time of War

After nearly 300 years, Mexico wanted its freedom from Spain. The Mexican War of Independence began in 1810 and lasted for 11 years. When it ended, Mexico won its freedom, and the Southwest no longer belonged to Spain.

In 1830, the president of the United States signed the Indian Removal Act. It forced American Indians to move from their homelands in the East. The government called the new home for native peoples Indian Territory. Later, some of this area became the state of Oklahoma.

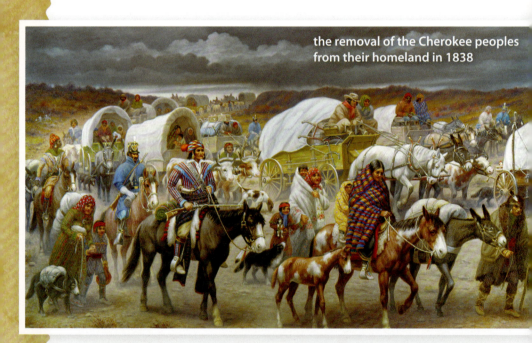

the removal of the Cherokee peoples from their homeland in 1838

### Meaning of Texas

The Caddo people lived in Texas when Spain arrived. Their word *taysha* means "friend." The Spanish people interpreted *taysha* as "the great kingdom of Tejas." Over time, Tejas (TEH-has) became Texas (TEX-us).

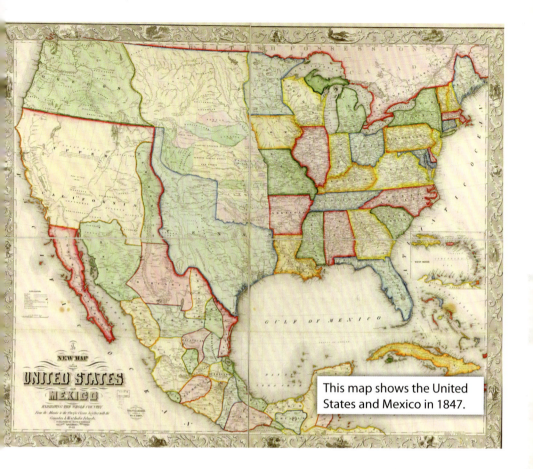

This map shows the United States and Mexico in 1847.

Mexico welcomed white settlers into Texas. At the time, there were just 3,500 settlers in Texas. Ten years later, the number had grown to 37,800!

But the new settlers wanted freedom from Mexico. A new war started—the Texas Revolution. It lasted for six months. The settlers won and formed the Republic of Texas. For 10 years, Texas was independent. It did not belong to Spain, Mexico, or the United States. In 1845, the people of Texas voted to join the United States as the 28th state.

But the United States and Mexico could not agree on the Texas borders. This dispute started the Mexican-American War. Through it, Mexico lost the lands of Arizona, New Mexico, and more. The current border of Texas was decided.

# American Civil War

In the 1860s, Texas was a state that allowed slavery. Cotton was a big crop in Texas, and enslaved people farmed it. There were hundreds of thousands of enslaved people in Texas. But the United States was working toward ending slavery. In 1861, Texas and 10 other states left the United States. They formed the **Confederate** States of America.

Indian Territory was not yet a state. But some American Indians did own enslaved people. There were between 8,000 and 10,000 enslaved people in Indian Territory. Some American Indians joined the Confederate Army. Civil War battles were fought in both Indian Territory and Texas.

The war ended in 1865. On June 19, 1865, slavery ended in Texas. This day has become known as Juneteenth. It is now a federal holiday. The people in Indian Territory ended slavery as well. Texas was ordered to rejoin the United States.

Oklahoma Land Rush

## Oklahoma Land Rush

The United States wanted people to settle in the area that became Oklahoma. In 1889, they held a race. The winners each got 160 acres (about 65 hectares) of land for free. About 50,000 people lined up to race. Only 12,000 of them could win. (Four more land runs took place between 1889 and 1895.)

The Oklahoma population skyrocketed. One month after the land race, Oklahoma City had five banks and six newspapers. This city had not existed a month before. In 1907, Oklahoma became the 46th state.

## Statehood

In 1903, the populations of Arizona and New Mexico were very small. Politicians tried combining the states to form one big state named Montezuma. The idea could not get enough votes in Congress, though. Both Arizona and New Mexico joined the United States in 1912.

# The Economy of the Land

Many of the riches from the Southwest come from its land. Oil, agriculture, and livestock are three of its biggest revenues. Texas produces the most oil in the nation. New Mexico and Oklahoma are high on the list of oil producers. Interestingly, Arizona does not have much oil at all. The state is near the bottom of the list for oil production. But several big companies have their headquarters in Arizona. That generates a lot of revenue for the state.

Texas is a very big state. It has more farms than any other state. It produces more cotton and hay than any other state. It also has the most cattle, horses, sheep, and goats. Texas earns more money than most countries in the world do.

The beautiful natural landscapes of New Mexico and Arizona make them big draws for tourism. The Grand Canyon, Painted Desert, Carlsbad Caverns, and more bring in tourists from all corners of the world. "Cowboy culture" in Oklahoma and Texas appeals to travelers. The famed Route 66 passes through all four states, and tourists still like to explore its interesting sites and scenes. Many people flock to Texas's famous cities, such as Dallas, Fort Worth, and Houston. The Gulf of Mexico is a popular tourist playground along the Texas coast. The city of Austin has a rich art and music scene that people love. And the San Antonio River Walk is a destination spot for many travelers.

## Smokey Bear

Smokey Bear was a small bear cub who climbed a tree to escape a New Mexico forest fire in 1950. His paws and legs had been burned. He was nursed back to health. Smokey Bear became the face of the Wildfire Prevention Campaign in the United States.

oil rigs and derricks in Oklahoma

cattle

the Grand Canyon and Colorado River

21

# Southwest Civics

People across the Southwest participate in their community lives. They vote, organize, and work together. They run for office, march for their causes, and protest what they think is not working. Like people across the country, they have an important say in how things are done.

People across the Southwest are proud of their communities and do what they can to care for them. They work to make things run well and to stay true to their values.

Many people of the Southwest are actively involved in public offices. In fact, several presidents of the United States have come from the Southwest. Lyndon B. Johnson was a high school teacher in Texas. In 1963, he became president of the United States. Johnson's grave and birthplace are located at the Lyndon B. Johnson National Historical Park in Stonewall, Texas.

George H. W. Bush and George W. Bush are father and son. Each has called Texas home. Both men have been president of the United States. It is only the second time in history that a father and son have both been president. George H. W. Bush died in 2018. He is buried at the George H. W. Bush Presidential Library and Museum, in College Station, Texas.

**President George H. W. Bush**

American Indian artists selling their goods at the Santa Fe Indian Market

## Important Presence

The states with the largest American Indian populations are Oklahoma, Arizona, New Mexico, and Texas, as well as California. More than ten percent of the populations of New Mexico and Oklahoma are American Indian peoples. A quarter of Arizona land is American Indian land. The voices of native peoples throughout the Southwest are important ones.

## From Tragedy to Triumph

In 2011, Gabby Giffords was a member of the U.S. Congress from Arizona. She was holding a rally at a shopping center. A man ran up to the crowd and began shooting a gun. He shot many people and killed several. Giffords was shot in the head but survived. Seven months later, she was back at work in Congress!

Giffords's husband is Mark Kelly. He was an astronaut. In 2020, he ran for the U.S. Senate in Arizona and won. Both Giffords and Kelly make gun laws a major part of their work.

former U.S. Representative Gabby Giffords and her husband Mark Kelly

### Tornado Alley

The nation's first tornado warning was issued in Oklahoma on March 25, 1948. Oklahoma has on average about 62 tornadoes each year, and Texas has about 155! Most of these tornadoes are small and do not cause much damage. But occasionally they can be deadly and very destructive to property. Important civic action in the Southwest includes preparing for natural disasters such as these and keeping communities safe.

Interior Secretary Deb Haaland is sworn into office.

## Leading the Way

In 2021, Deb Haaland became the first American Indian to serve as a U.S. **cabinet** secretary. Haaland was born in Arizona. Today, she reports to the president of the United States. She is responsible for public land and water. This is a big deal. American Indians have long wanted their homelands and water returned to them. But most of the time, they have been kept from positions of leadership in the country. Haaland is breaking barriers and making a difference.

## The Future Is Now

Across the Southwest, spaceports are being built. They are built there because it is easier to get a rocket into space closer to the equator. Many people are working toward this dream.

Perhaps most famous is Jeff Bezos. He was the second person in the world to have one hundred billion dollars. Bezos was born in New Mexico. Later, he was raised in Texas. Since he was five years old, Bezos has dreamed about flying into outer space. He started a company that builds rockets. In 2021, he completed a rocket that took him and his brother into outer space. The rocket launched from Texas.

## Keeping the Past Alive

The Southwest is a beautiful land. It is steeped in history but looks to the future. Culture is an important part of its story, and culture keeps its history alive. It remembers the builders of the ancient pueblos that still stand. It remembers a history with Spain and Mexico. It honors the traditions of the American Indians who first lived across the land. And it celebrates those who look toward the stars.

The Southwest has its challenges. But there is one thing history has shown the world—the Southwest will survive and thrive.

### Spain's Legacy

Many people throughout the Southwest speak Spanish. Nearly one-third of the people in New Mexico speak Spanish at home. The same is true for Texans. And about one-fifth of Arizona residents consider Spanish their home language.

Downtown San Antonio, Texas

# Map It!

The U.S. government removed many American Indian tribes from their homelands. They moved them to Indian reservations. These reservations are located on land that the United States did not necessarily see as valuable. The land was often located far from their tribal homes. But on Indian reservations, a tribe is an independent nation. They are separate from the state or federal government.

There are currently 326 Indian reservations in the United States. The largest is the Navajo Nation in the Southwest.

Make a map showing some of the reservations of the Southwest.

1. Research to find which tribes have reservations in the Southwest.
2. Draw a map showing the locations of these tribes.
3. Think about the following questions as you research:

    - Which state has the most reservations?
    - Which state has the fewest?
    - Why do you think that is?

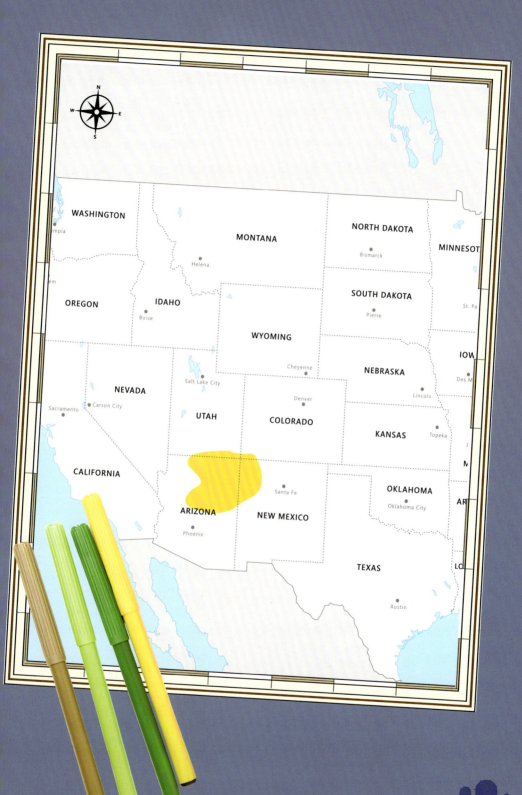

# Glossary

**buttes**—steep hills with flat tops

**cabinet**—a group of people who give advice to the leader of a government

**canals**—devices used to move water long distances to supply fields and crops with water

**Confederate**—relating to the 11 U.S. states that seceded during the Civil War

**conquistador**—a leader in the Spanish conquests of the Americas

**customs**—behaviors that are usual and traditional among people in a particular group or area

**diverse**—made up of people or things that are different from one another

**heritages**—traditions that are a part of the history of a group

**immunity**—the power to resist infection from a virus or disease

**indigenous**—from or native to a particular area

**lariat**—a stiff rope that is used as a lasso

**lasso**—a rope with a loop that is used for catching animals

**mission control**—the group of people on the ground who direct the flight of a spacecraft

**NASA**—National Aeronautics and Space Administration

**Paleo-Indians**—the earliest human inhabitants of the Americas

**reef**—a chain of coral and rocks along a shoreline

**spaceport**—a base from which spacecrafts are launched

**spurs**—sharp objects attached to horse riders' boots that are used to make the horse go faster

**squash**—a hard-skinned vegetable that is usually cooked and then eaten

**stirrups**—loops that are attached to a saddle for the rider's feet

# Index

American Civil War, 18

American Indians, 4, 8–13, 15–16, 18, 23, 25–26

Bush, George H. W., 22

Bush, George W., 22

Canyon de Chelly, 10

Chaco Canyon, 11

Colorado River, 7, 14, 21

Congress, 19, 24

Coronado, Francisco Vázquez de, 14–15

Giffords, Gabby, 24

Grand Canyon, 7, 14, 20–21

Haaland, Deb, 25

Hohokam, 10

Indian Territory, 16, 18

Johnson, Lyndon B., 22

Johnson Space Center, 5

Juneteenth, 18

Kelly, Mark, 24

Mexican-American War, 17

Mexican War of Independence, 16

Mexico, 8–9, 14, 16–17, 20, 26

Montezuma, 19

Oklahoma City, 19

Oklahoma Land Rush, 19

Paleo-Indians, 10

Spain, 8–9, 14–17, 26

Sunset Crater, 10

Texas Revolution, 17

Tornado Alley, 24

31

# Learn More!

There are many American Indians in the world today. The 2010 U.S. census showed that more than 5.2 million people identified as American Indians. Some are famous scientists, musicians, or writers. Others could be your next-door neighbors.

Many American Indians live in the Southwest. Research someone alive today who belongs to an American Indian tribe in the Southwest. Perhaps they are a politician, an actor, or an astronaut. Maybe they are mentioned in this book.

- ✦ Discover what tribe they belong to.

- ✦ Plan and design a wall mural that shows their life story. Draw your ideas on paper. Feature their accomplishments. Include the history of their tribe.

- ✦ Write a short paragraph that tells who the person is and what is shown in your mural.

Navajo Family outside their home In Monument Valley Tribal Park, Utah